Oil Slick Dreams

poems by

Jennifer L. Collins

Finishing Line Press
Georgetown, Kentucky

Oil Slick Dreams

Copyright © 2016 by Jennifer L. Collins
ISBN 978-1-944899-33-2 First Edition
All rights reserved under International and Pan-American Copyright Conventions. No part of this book may be reproduced in any manner whatsoever without written permission from the publisher, except in the case of brief quotations embodied in critical articles and reviews.

ACKNOWLEDGMENTS

A number of these poems were first published by small magazines and journals, and I'd like to thank all of those publications for their support.

"Nighttime Warnings" was first published in *Redivider*.
"Fairy Tale Shadows" was first published in *The Potomac Review*.
"Easier" was first published in *34th Parallel*.
"Roadkill" was first published in *Puerto Del Sol*.
"Echoes in Friends" was first published in *Redactions: Poetry, Poetics, & Prose*.
"Knots of Grace" was first published in *Ayris Magazine*.
"Figurations" and "Behind You" were first published in *The Kudzu Review*.
"So to Speak" and "Taking Down Pictures" were first published by *Collective Exile*.
The second section of "Visions Elsewise" was published under the title "Sideways Equals" by *Fjords*.

For their support, their friendship, and their inspiration, I also owe endless thanks to my friends and family, especially to my mom Pat Collins, my grandmother Mercedes Tuggle, and to Joel Gorman, Jeff Stoyanoff, Nicola Brooke, Julie Aronson, James Pittman, John Fried, Keith Morris, Ryan G. Van Cleave, Brad Baker, Adam Million, F. Simon Grant, Matt Rinkin, Devin Clifford, Samantha Freese, Jack Foster, Miller Clifford, and RJ Gorman.

Publisher: Leah Maines
Editor: Christen Kincaid
Cover Art: James Pittman, http://jamespittmangallery.com/
Author Photo: Joel Gorman
Cover Design: Elizabeth Maines

Printed in the USA on acid-free paper.
Order online: www.finishinglinepress.com
        also available on amazon.com

Author inquiries and mail orders:
Finishing Line Press
P. O. Box 1626
Georgetown, Kentucky 40324
U. S. A.

Table of Contents

Nighttime Warnings 1

A Locking of Sight 2

Fairy Tale Shadows 3

Easier 5

Roadkill 7

Legends Fishing for Horizons 8

Echoes in Friends 9

Knots of Grace 10

inside hope 11

Figurations 12

Behind You 13

Spoken For 14

Taking Down Pictures 15

Visions Elsewise: A Sequence 16

Meaning Broken 34

Under Clouds 35

*Dedicated to my Dad,
Tom W. Collins*

Nighttime Warnings

Be careful of the moonbeams.
Bleeding romance on the carpet,
looking like trails of angel feathers,
they've been lying there waiting
for you to come home.

It's just the moon,
scientifically shedding light
through the panes of glass and lines
of wood that shelter you in
and keep out the night.
You don't notice the danger
in the glitter on burgundy shag
that only seems golden in downtime,
and so you don't remember either
that the glitter never notices you.
If you close the shade,
those angel footsteps won't
tempt you to dream into their wingways,
brown will be brown beneath
the tight shoes on your feet.
The lights will do the trick
as well if you turn them on quickly—
no need to imagine the pretend magic
that you think might be there
in the lighted squares.

Just remember to be careful
of the moonbeams waiting for you,
dripping out dreams and tussling desire and being
unpractical there on your floor, there praying
on you where you can't help but see them.

A Locking of Sight

In empty playing fields,
memories and possibilities negotiate
for space in the present.
>   Our eyes watch both shadow groups,
>   spilling desire and remedying what little
>   hope remains in split-second decisions.

It doesn't matter that the fields are still frozen,
players still slipping from bed or, if tenacious,
perhaps warming muscles on sidewalks and in parks.

It doesn't matter that eyes alone are flitting
over the day's coming mistakes and passes,
or that possibilities, unfound, may be realer than
>   what's to come,
>   dreams realer than tomorrows,
>   eventualities treading harder than time.

Invented memories may be just as fashionable as the real thing,
if given time to foster truth and mature: either can lead
to the same solid structure, or an equally charred truth.

In empty playing fields,
no team glory or heart breaking
yet matters or holds court.
>   And, too, eyes can drift over truths to
>   determine presence, determine new hopes
>   for a field of something less.

Fairy Tale Shadows

At eight, I knew the name Afghanistan.
I could spell it and find it on a map,
would speak endlessly of the far-off place
      —I dreamed of it—
that held the most significant beauty I'd seen,
could imagine at that age:
a cat, snow leopards.

Knowing they were endangered, hunted,
I dreamed of helping them,
of living in those mountains
and convincing others they weren't worth fighting
      —let alone killing—
the majesty of their lives just something else
to show us the beauty of our own world:
price of pelt aside, poverty of people aside,
I pictured them just below heaven.

Now involuntarily, my mind makes the same association.
News of war, of hiding, of fear and starvation,
and I think of those cats, my childhood vision
still waiting in the background on my panel of thoughts.
I can tell you, if you want to know, that they
are more hunted now than before,
their pelts protected as their skin
and hearts are stripped of life,
blood dribbling down muscle without skin they lost
      —to the Taliban, for warmth and for money—
but then, so are our soldiers searched out,
and so it means only so much to even my eyes.

With poverty and lives and injustice in the balance,
an endangered cat seems of little consequence in the light.
Yet, we didn't crawl from Plato's caves of shadows to find
fear and famine only in our foremost perceptions
      —I tell myself we have the right to fight This—
and we should not show maps to children simply
so they'll understand war, or hate. Through this,
my clichéd heart argues that the cat I always thought of,
on some level, is still worth my consideration
      —separate from the terror—

and that our work should be that each of us is able
to crawl from whatever caves of shadows we've inhabited,
that this begets peace,
finding our mountains, our snow leopards,
our Afghanistans.

Easier

First grade friends were easy to come by—
a weasel named Montgomery who stole the dog's food
and told jokes about balloons,
a white wolf named Bambi who loved to watch *Thundercats*
and told bedtime stories,
an anteater named Janelle who'd get paint everywhere
and do anything for chocolate,
a komodo dragon named Robert who helped us dig for treasure
and liked to see-saw better than swing—
all loyal and right to trust,
always available,
never truly hurt or hurting back.

Already invisible,
they became less visible with time,
and I slowly forgot to call on them,
no matter how I needed
or wanted them
to be there.
Other friends were louder,
certainly more real,
and the invisibles
held back.
As reliable as ever, though,
they left me
when asked,
neglected
out of existence,
and even out of memory.

A thousand firsts later—
drinking liquored up grape-fruit juice instead
of apple juice or milk,
smoking chained together Parliament lights instead
of sucking on pixie sticks,
hanging with dozens of sidelong acquaintances instead
of knowing a few best friends,
grading papers in front of the Jon Stewart show instead
of dozing in front of *Dumbo*,
balancing a checkbook for food on the table
instead of begging quarters for gum—
I stand in the quarter of a friend's party,
perched on the bench of a picnic table,
forgotten myself for the moment,

and wish for one of them
to reappear, however invisible
they couldn't help being.

Road Kill

Twitch, avenue.
> (tempt me to teeter and fall drunken to the floor like the scattered froth from a slobbard's worshipped Fosters)

I can lie
> (incoherently on your soft asphalt, allow lost exaggerations of pity, pain, need to escape lipstick lined levers of love and anger)

We both know
> (men mingle desire and devotion with tactical warfare, rebelling from Aphrodite's manifesto to allow the abolition of a nymphet's evolution)

You cradle
> (with concrete quickly at a tipped glance, closer than a kiss, intimately instigating bruises, carrying ecstasy in simple harsh acceptance)

I can fall
> (as I have, glasses smeared, make-up broken, jewelry jangling report to entice passing applicants to malice)

They can watch
> (me recline on your black pathway of heat and oil and muck waiting for rubber to pave over and through me with a man's fierce negligence)

I'll live
> (some 'til then out of spite out of tilting despairing comprehension and pray penitently for a little death)

Twitch, Avenue.

Legends Fishing for Horizons

Like the oiled waters had carried them all the way out into the Gulf,
like the waters had driven and deserted them ahead, angrily, and forced them
    toward the horizon line,
like the waters were a burgeoning war, working against peace with brutal eyes,
and like there was no space left behind them,
the fishermen drifted one by one to sea.

Professional fishing gear left behind or forgotten on decks in favor of single
    simple rod and reel,
pitying neighbors and family left in favor of unwarring waters
    and silent starshine,
the fishermen left with many things, but without looking back.

They carried no oil, but sails and oars.
They carried no pets, but some brought recovering pelicans
    and other creatures, worn dry
        from oil, and resting now in human hands.
They carried no pieces of landed nature, but some
    brought photographs of pristine waters,
        blue horizons, or watered
            memories to drive their search.
They carried little food, but much water.
They carried dead dreams, and live ones.

Following the strength of the horizon,
they fled chaos singly, one by one,
none admitting aloud that leaving their forever
    home would be forever,
none admitting that the happy endings of yesterday
    had ended, as a life and as a world.
They fled, becoming a fairy tale legend in themselves,
gliding in peace, in terror, in tortured-out acceptance.

And those behind them,
left on a different land than that the fishermen had fled,
guessed they had died searching out cleaner waters,
but dreamed of an accepting horizon,
of renewed men and unoiled waters,
unoiled waters which carried no harm,
harbored no manufactured brutality,
and meant no chase to come
or danger toward dreams.

Echoes in Friends
for J.S. & N.B.

A staircase of memories
   descends   violently
escalating me into your history,
one that darkens down
from   my sight
into what might be known
and treasured.

Each footstep down
   cracked with my fear
of attachment,
the path is no more
clear   in love
than it would be in hatred.
Tripping down
   I am dusted with frost
of memory   you've hidden
from sight, even sound.

Each step is countless,
each footfall light
   —light I believe—
on the borders
of your staircase,
memoried   into mind,
another layer to be mindful
of   or   or forget—
I fear
being memoried into this
   staircase,
out of sight, under mind.

These are crooked stairs:
   haunted   pleasantly cracked.
Descending,
I ascend my own,
each step   into your care
one
   more footfall
     down,
        into mine.

Knots of Grace

What looks like prayer stills
the coffee I was about to pour,
slipping a breath of meditation
into my movement to you.

In your solitude, I realize
    I should not be able to expect you at this moment.
    I should not know this is your favorite shirt, even with the stained sleeve.
    I should not know the green in your right eye, not your left.

What looks like prayer tickles my throat
and I freeze my teeth against a cough
or an awkward grin that could interrupt
this before I move to you.

In your clenched hands, I see clearly,
    I should not feel the breath of my heart or the presence of each footfall.
    I should not wonder about the slant of my hair or my faded apron.
    I should not see my shadows more than your progression.

What looks like prayer stills me
to ask whether this coffee is
for last night or today,
your past, or my present.

inside hope

Could a prayer work like sweat
against God's skin?

Forming from prayers, each one
a slip of moisture from
an almighty pore
being affected by the simple
and honest breath of a believer.

I can imagine bronze skin
glistening aloud with the words
of a thousand fathers of sons at war,
a thousand sons and daughters,
the hundreds who sit waiting
by beds or by phones, in company,
or alone.

I can see sweat beaded and cold
at the nape of Mary's neck,
in the crook of her arm,
and I can even pretend
that the moisture in my bangs
is evaporating towards hers
as I pray upward.

If a prayer is concrete
when it reaches Heaven,
if it beads like sweat,
if it turns cold like the breath
of a Ghost in waiting,
I could believe my
way to faith.

Figurations

Spiderman, baby
    (all tied up with sewing thread, half sprawled in a pond, webbed out
    by some demented five year old and subject to rain, snow, mud more
    dangerous than the villainy he's meant to take on)
there layin' in the dust
    (holdin' out for some Peter-Pan rescue of youth or magic with the snow
    comin' down and the red and the blue—the vibrant stuff, see—all
    covered in the gray muck of daylight)
like the way I wait
    (your headlights somewhere off in the distance, countin' the miles away
    from any webs I ever spun, on you or anyone, your foot on the gas,
    some little MJ Watson feminist on a power trip)
with my webs
    (or any ability to spin for you, for me, all wrapped up in the waiting,
    counting, hoping on my heroine who's just trying to hold herself out of
    the rain when I could lay groundwork for survival if not)
all tied up in you
    (in your vision instead of functioning in or at least seeing mine here
    already spread over our world only limited by imposed structure
    with the strength of sewing thread because of you I'm all tied up)
like some tired action figure, baby.

Behind You

Blood comes from the muse quietly,
dyeing the soil beneath her and thickening
between blades of grass—
above the groove, headlights slide by
unseeing, unseen,
too high and practical to illuminate
any entity in any ditch.
In a fold of her limp gypsy skirt,
her cell phone twitches for a hand
in the fair silence, unused
to being ignored or forgotten.

The calls coming in,
second-guessing a murderer's hand,
are constant.

Even the murderer calls once,
somewhat in hope of an answer,
something in denial of death,
but it's a lightning bug who lands finally
and first on her still touch to mourn,
his soft whir reaching out in anger
to cover the blank of her eyes.

Spoken For

nighttime on the telephone,
with a whisper of logic,
says "i am alone"

Close to the hold of the telephone,
nighttime whispers to the day
of being alone, fingers
splayed on thighs
and tapping a silent rhythm,
bored silent.

Calling up logic,
nighttime looks for friendship
in imagination, in self-reflection,
in identity,
and considers Eve beneath her tree,
nobody more alone
as her Adam sleeps in the distance
and round reds beckon in quiet.

In this dream finally
nighttime is unalone,
comforted by a rising color
on the horizon

Taking Down Pictures

"If I am crazy,"
    whispers nighttime, "what is the day?"

Fingers splayed painfully on thighs,
nighttime sits near a telephone,
waiting for answers
every day
alone.

"Think of Adam, sleeping restlessly
    while Eve gazes at bright fruits
    and dreams more vividly"

A silent rhythm runs through the night's mind,
tapping upon cells that can encompass
the color of day, and waiting,
while near all of the world
worships at daytime's
dusted heels.

"While he dreamt in his own night,
    Eve was discovering sin, and infatuation,
    in her own daytime—
    and so we follow in her footsteps?"

Walking away from landlines, the nighttime
begins slowly to take down all pictures,
leaving only blank walls for company
as moments of indulgence
are turned backward.

"Worshipping daytime discoveries,
    and yet all still wait for me, for comfort,
    looking for windows into mystery."

Cracking in doors, loosening latches to windows,
attempting an arrest of the average logic,
nighttime moves slowly before resting
near glimpses of daylight, watching
for new sightings of delight,
or at least of waking
pictures of sin
or patience.

Visions Elsewise: A Sequence

1

Somewhere else another two a.m. heartbreak
    (she sitting curled in his couch like roadkill dropped carelessly,
    beaten eyes blinking out shock in now expectant moonlight this
    was known today this was known yesterday still she sits curled in
    his couch like roadkill)
with dawn far out of sight and somewhere else
    (he details a made-up mugging to the emergency room doctor
    believes him being a him the eyes of each man feigning proper
    feeling when he stumbles shocked thinking this is the third
    emergency room he's running out of unknown hospitals)
with love waiting outside and somewhere else
    (this is the first time second time third time fourth time fifth time
    perhaps with eyes full of anger unobserved as other eyes turn
    downward fear becoming a subspecies of love love becoming
    synonymous with regret)
when at four a.m. in somewhere else
    (she cleans the space around her quietly he sleeps upstairs eyes
    peaceful dreaming just so much as hers scatter the floor for the
    last last-night's left over bits of anger to be disposed of as if seen
    again they'll only bring more action)
toward dawn in somewhere else
    (when he leans back into the passenger seat to leave behind new
    doctors with his lover hater driving eyes forward always again
    words spoken before nights before no need for them again
    though they'll come again)
always promising something else.

2

Anymore, he remembers pain
no differently than love,
either cranberry colored passion
just a twist away from disgust
in the tired sight of this future,
and only a turn away from swollen eyes
full away with tears that might
still be coming,
however long ago they began to form.

Last night's innocent blister pangs
in tandem with a bruised shoulder
—uninnocent— and timed to
the distance on his lover's lips,
just so bitten back as the glaze
over once known eyes.
His thumb against the side
of a cold glass, waiting for relief
that could not only alleviate,
but erase from memory
for better or worse
any sting at all.

He wants to ask a balm for sight and heart,
sympathy, sitting
one thumb twitching
for other pains,
and no second heart to beat commiseration
for one quietly breaking.

But eyes as dark as before,
walled against regret—
they signal no change, no true promise,
and still he'd take the sting of burst skin
over the blunt lack of look across from him,
brought on by this request,
even if the pains are forever unable to heal.

The blister has started to heal,
of course,

with a slight background ache,
and he was never offered a choice of pains.
There's no surprise there, though,
for even from the beginning,
sight bound in pain and love,
he knew which passion would be stronger,
and which would be the one to heal.

3

She imagines things
even when he's not there.
In one night's breath,
here his nail gliding along the skin
          of her forearms, her palms,
his cobra eyes slick against hers.
In another night's whisper,
she nearly feels the thump of a fist
          here on her cheek,
worse if she stays or she goes
she can't know.

She could ignore his presence as we do,
tell herself she should and move beyond
the curse of the dreams in mind,
even if into an unknown future
of poverty or luck.

The problem is, his name fits
here on her lips, in her breath.
His name sleeps trained on her tongue
even when he leaves the room,
even when her mind should be stationed
          in the day, away from his
          hello or goodnight.

His sway in time,
his sight on her self,
his knowing gaze to accompany
a nail or a fist on her skin
          —as imagined
          these the possibilities that hold breath—
exchanges comfort for security,
forces her belief that a perhaps safe now
is more right than an unsafe later,
pushes her to accept another day,
another day,
as forgotten,
as imagined.

4

In the view of a jealousy born lens,
his world stumbles out of breath
in waiting for a lover's clearer sight.
Visions of a past's imaginings
hold his ground steady
enough for waiting in balance.

His is a limp born of madness
he's grown accustomed to,
moving forward in a vein of hope
and surrendering in patience.
His movement in the shades of an other's
forgetful forgiveness and unforgiving love
echoes the lurch in his eyes
when confronted with strangers,
forewarns of the blank sight
he meets in home's breath.

Waiting with a devil's patience,
pushed into a game of guilt and anger,
his eyes are still untuned to change,
unready for the unexpected
fall from grace born
steep before him.

5

Step down then into questioning
    the seen pairs of power play
        built around downturned
            eyes already silent.

Watch for the waiting
    journeymen, journeywomen
        blinking toward daylight
            for the possibility
                of some release.

Make a wish on the eyelashes
    dipped in blood and dipped in tears
        waiting in quiet view on fingertips
            for a fantasy undecided.

Time the sighted repercussions
    by which any individual
        is built to be an inhuman
            production of power
                on and over another.

Observe agency taken
    over by one's force on
        another out of energy
            until questions intervene.

Reword the world so far
    constructed in static
        individuals of strength or or or
            only weakness
                for a journey decided

6

It's a quiet wound,
resting without pretense
      upper on her cheekbone
      blue beneath seeing eyes
      oval and jarring in its peace
      like a third eye
as if it has always been there
waiting on interpretation.

Watching elsewhere,
her vision clouds over the world
she knows around her,
spacing others' visions into a separateness
she need not acknowledge.
Feet away, others watch her there,
peripherally interested in her
separation and quiet,
disquieting their own views.

The bruise after all is bold,
more so beneath her meekening eyes,
vises clamping what's left of
pride and fading
above the color on her breasted cheek,
their empty sight out of focus,
but clear enough
to break
the surface of peaceful eyes around her, and
still proud enough to maintain silence.

7

Ever, is this the feminine he searches for?
Her silenced eyes buried against the wall,
nails pulsing against skin like eyelids shut
black against pain?

His curious sight locked on her submission
suggests the cycle is reinforced here,
a culture within a hall of
        emotions that grow quietly,
        perspectives so real as to be
        stereotyped, unexamined,
        a fourth world holding steady
        behind progression
a tangent of the future she once dreamed,
and left behind.

His construction,
this vision her eyes have
sunken down to accept,
has re-made her world
through the blackmail piecemeal journey
        of his praise,
        his darkened view,
        his clenched control
enclosing her bitten nails.

Slivers of fight in the carpets,
broken art underfoot,
survival now a mission of subjection
in his approving eyes
bent on her hunched identity.
This is in sight his view
of the feminine, without
multiple perspective, without
        question.

8

Faith swept away so easily as ashes,
his eyes on elsewhere,
my neighbor grows adept at delusions
with each move of his lover
in his background.

At square one, they had difference tied
        between them,
shadowed together by appropriated affection.
Reaching beyond hope to another space in outside eyes,
no exit considered with the future in sight,
material surroundings disappeared
in favor of love, their version of truth.

He can't remember when this ended,
but I remember a broken night,
his figure sleepless, hunched,
out-of-habit smoking on his porch
as the sun rose and I went for the paper.

I think that each second counted that morning
in my wave of greeting unanswered.

I think that he saw crossroads flashing
in immediate memory on his night before,
        on that morning,
as light rose on ashes.
That night, I believe, is when one lover's
fist hit brick inside flesh,
found a fault line in a backstreet of dreams
unsighted so far, unrepaired.

I didn't expect to find this figure in him,
or for that first morning to haunt
my sight when I see him there in the mornings
that seem darker now,
shaded with both ashes and bruised skin
in slight non-sleeping recovery.

9

Her scars starved for meaning
    (in my sight waiting for validation perhaps the shapes the same
    another left her the same she'll live with tomorrow waiting for
    meaning or an outsider's justice of thought while the balance of her
    grey eyes tips scales of hope)
burning and recognized
    (speckled, tearing edges raw centered with blistering beginnings a
    dirty pink that reminds unfashionably inappropriately of sex where
    they came from perhaps the meanings and scars interchangeable now
    as her my eyes tilt down)
to avoid judgement
    (the space of my skin burnished by nature alone and hers marked
    by affection turned love turned something else somewhere else in a
    currency of attachment moved from tender illusion into delusions
    dripping from sleepbroken nights)
Her scars and her hope
    (the same vision now nearly moving from raw action to a waiting on
    flesh and on spirit to move or to be moved by circumstance or love
    a lack of love drifting over silenced foresight now hiding itself in
    memory tangled in)
counted in layers
    (visible to anyone both sensual and picked at wounds for months
    scabs for weeks layered over with each touch hers and another's still
    now visible to any eyes chancing by offering judgment sympathy
    denial pause)
to eat at memories of
    (something better still visible perhaps I guess in her eyes since the
    leaving hasn't begun not from the dip in her chin the dark glasses the
    light bag clutched loosely the fingertips still hovering silently
    stuttering over scars and hope)
waiting to heal.

10

Whether you've led me or left me to a dawn-bound sky
   —which I can't reach for the handcuffs you've given me—
or not,
the view here of suffering is grand.

In the backlights of your eyes this dead to others,
I can still see the moment of invitation toward flying upward
when I agreed in shade that your hand
offered more than torment,
that your words
   —chemicals—
could mean more than wobbling stilts or snowbanks.

On this cliff cut off from sky,
where dawn for myself is bound out of view by your chains,
suffering from here is everywhere understood,
as lurid as the mean notes in a Dada song,
the tortured breath of Stein
or the hard breath of a heart just fallen.

Whether, then, you've led me and left me to a dawn-bound sky
   —which I can't reach for the handcuffs you've gifted me—
or not,
I'm satisfied now reaching only my view
and being here, always before dawn,
breathing for these tremors of being understood.

11

Of course the managing happens in the nighttime,
settling life while children sleep undreaming,
thoughts silent since dreams could only bleed
into lifelike nightmares.

His thoughts never drift to their dreams,
no more venturing there than his hand
would advent a caress of his woman's cheek.
Not to be thought about or considered,
the skin,
pale and unmade in most daylights,
pinked up with fuller lips in the evening for his sight,
and reddened with tears or pain
when the light switch
hits the down place,
and her man sees warm color as only simply
a dark space of target and convenience
for hold, for halt.

On occasion, the class ring jars against cheekbone,
and gem casing leaves a crimson crease
along paled skin, perhaps a smear upon gold and blue
that will wash away with aftershave, in tomorrows.

Her thoughts focus on these tomorrows,
thinking a crease or a smear might signal regret
in the mornings, the mornings
after management.
In those mornings, she allows for his good words
to lead the younger ones through and out of home,
for good words to brew coffee
and ignore the presence that she has, still, regardless,
and that he's spent the night troubling out of attention.

Time past, she'll rise into her manager's shadows
and begin re-sembling the home keeper
he sought out with a gold ring on her finger.
For time coming, she'll pretend toward control,
and the children will look toward listening to her voice
rather than his louder shadow,
and in the evening things will appear honed,
the perfect description of home, family, beloved chaos.

And in the night, both the dreams and the nightmares
are well-managed, tucked beneath laundered sheets,
and kept silent, without any troubling.
No management can be observed, no orchestration,
no integration of one's want under another's.
Her skin just becomes uncreased, unreddened for segments
of moments awaiting, untiring, his touch,
for the paled skin of unmanaged mornings is less alive,
less colorful and less noticed, in truth,
than the pinkened skin that he sometimes cares enough
to create, to manage, to feel,
and she is surely less alive in the days
and evenings before
than in the tarnished mornings after.

12

        the difference between the hold on a hand and a wrist
              discovered only afterward, hindsighted
           into existence as one feels pain for the other
           one clenches back   one can only be led
one breathes simply, comforted   one frozen at a pinched nerve
         one able to slip free   one held at narrowest bend
             the difference here at meeting point
          between two walkers, connected in space
             a symptom of love and of power
            one rests equally   one held in careful sway
      one recognizes resistance   one with dictated expectations
 one swings quiet in unified trust   one enmeshed in control
             the difference here between two holds
               one of a hand and one of a wrist
                   nearly identical in sight
             and opposite in strength, in tenure

13

Hollow intentions
whispered softly
beneath souled-out grey eyes:
prodding in quiet rooms. Hostility

hidden for the time,
he's still begging for chances
"only this one time"
with moistened glances window-way.

Both know one-more-chances
aren't supposed to last
more than minutes, days—
long enough to subtly cast

doubt on tears that make hard
bruises seem small,
bets on careful change,
new starts, a new fall down

forward into him again,
into a past turned future and
known already too well
by love's doe-eyed afterglow end

of purple black tints.
One more chance, moving on,
afforded as before once more for
one more moment on, and on.

14

Trapeze-dweller eyes,
    balanced against fate,
        she slides to the side of his fist
            with a practice born harshly

    ——here, your line, here, for balance——

Toe to instep, she perches poised
    like a child for bolting,
        acknowledging through a lens of old love that
            this balancing act is all hers,
                each sway a bob into fear,
                      each non-step a sighted dismissal of the same

    ——balancing here, without bruise, in his sight——

In a niche of constant recovery,
    balanced against fate,
        her eyes feint against his fist,
            out of practice a-sudden at each impact

    ——out of balance, here, out of balance——

15

Dragon eyes and rum breath
bearing through the windows,
your thoughts hitting mine with a force.

You see just blush on the pillow I left
now here gleaming my cheek;
I see dark bruises beneath the same blush
left there, hanging in check.

Maybe it looks like rainbows to you,
purple and blue against pink,
the tears there for light
and eye shadow for green
and the rainbow to take out the bite.

For me they were dog bites,
just burning and tinted
with rum and with care and with hate,
but as rainbows in your eyes
and artworks in your hands
      —the cracks of the ribs and the breaking of skin,
      the rainbows, the rushes, the cries out within—
they blossomed to branches of hate.

So as your thoughts hit mine
with the force of those rainbows
and your fists clench wild as you beg,
I can look through these windows
at my dragon with rum breath
and take on your sight,
for the freedom in my head.

16

Somewhere else, aren't they
    (the grieving sockets structured, embalmed by bruises and
    insomniactic fears in man woman child eyes everywhere as
    confronted with apparent love's fists, burns, hates(?) could be
    extended here in shadow)
such hates distributed by love
    (channeled through violence, governed by circumstance just
    outside of the picture-perfected vision of society, politically
    correct in another time, hidden or ignored or unwatched or or or
    or or by most in the present)
Stage combat idealized
    (observed in a way here, it's the victim who does the work in
    waiting watching backpedaling feeling understanding the
    dynamics of what did does will happen even as guilt)
guards against change
    (guilt unreasoned just seasoned by pain and hope for love's
    bindings, real or imagined, to unbind pained history in favor of
    what should be—perhaps? correct?—or could in a righter world)
with stars hidden under hurt
    (battling silence silently civilly in an uncivil presentation of love
    unworlded unfostered, perpetrated instead it seems out of greed
    power sullen tradition at times of course too common in each
    exchange)
Burdened out of freedom
    (the faded stars expected to escape to help themselves to demand
    wisdom or escape, humanity at least, out of bondage unthankless
    for a waiting world as observers watch quieted by self-dignity
    unknown by)
still fading stars
    (who know despair out of hope and the feared exile from a
    lover's threat—in mind if not body—persistent in each act of
    authority experienced consistently more powerful with each
    mis-under-stood raised hand)
bend toward violence
    (collapsing beneath a web of waiting observers—obedient only
    to falsely leading love's expectations—love's apparent combats
    savage and cracked in sight, hope, waiting, wisdom)
wisdom weighting waiting

Meaning Broken

I see your tongue flicker
from out of your lips,
thoughtful and unaware,
and I know the meaning.

I know you don't know what to say,
or even where you stand in the breadth of discussion,
that you'd rather now be reclining at your desk
or alone, driving, no next moment to consider.

Your tongue rests along the ridge of your upper lip,
your head and mind shaking in tune, uncaring—
the next moment of unknowing means less than the last,
and that less than the one before.

Lost in your indecision, my own words
clutter out of sight to return later
when the moments are less pressing,
and less aware of your pursed lips,
waiting for escape, and catering
to my imagination,
too aware of what you mean.

Under Clouds
    for M.C.

lying beside you, I think perhaps
I was meant to be a dog before a poet,
a pack animal instead of a girl.
puppy calls sounding more like language
than worded discussions on the distance.
clarity under clouds coming with whimpers
from dog to master, heartbeat to soul.

you lean on me for comfort
traded likewise between us,
body heat and compassion just such
treasured commodities as love
when I consider the afternoon's peace
even under the weight
of our separate yearnings.
it's true my knowledge means
nothing confronted by these emotions on hold,
companionship making more sense than art.

I can hear the countering against the afternoon's peace,
that a pup can make no poet,
that potential comes with the favor of humanity,
that the compassion built into simple presence,
heartbeat against heartbeat,
is only imagined, nothing more
than pillow for body, escape for mind.

but animals so often make more sense,
rescuing one another and us as if they knew better
the definition of shelter,
of the cry for care, *rescue me*,
heard echoing on air,
as if to suggest that meaning
comes only with one life's
breathed response
felt simply to another.

Jennifer grew up in Richmond, VA., where much of her time was devoted to writing and theater. As a Junior in college at Shenandoah University, she began sending out her work for publication. Over the years since then, her poems have found homes in dozens of national and international publications, and the pursuit of poetry has found her in all sorts of different positions where she never envisioned herself.

While pursuing a MA at Clemson University, she helped with open mics, worked on organizing a reading series (serving as MC more often than she would have liked...), and helped to organize a weekly group for writers that met for more than four years. After teaching for a few years at Clemson, she moved on to Pittsburgh, thinking that a PhD was the next step. Instead, a number of things happened. While working on her ill-fated PhD, she began working as the Poetry Editor and later the Editor of the school's literary and arts journal, *:lexicon*. She also began editing full-length manuscripts on a full-time basis. Perhaps most importantly, she was contacted by Shenandoah University about developing a Creative Writing branch for their summer performing arts camp for high school students. Developing the course, and then co-teaching the 14-day intensive program for two summers, was some of the most fulfilling work she'd done up to that point.

Over the next few years, Jennifer found herself spending more time editing, encouraging artists around her university in Pittsburgh, working with young writers in her community, and organizing a much-needed art show on her campus, which has now run annually for four years, though she left the university in Spring of 2014. At the same time, she began working as a Creative Writing and Drama teacher at the Cardigan Mountain School in Canaan, NH. during their summer sessions. Now, although she's relocated to Florida and works as a book editor for most of the year, she still spends her summers teaching at Cardigan, and hopes to begin organizing after-school programs for young writers in her new community.

This is her first published collection of poetry. She lives with her husband of five years in Cape Coral, FL., where they've got a house full of rescues— one neurotic hound dog, one one-eyed long-haired tortoiseshell, and two rambunctious younger cats who found their way into their home. She writes every day, works with writers every day, and is thankful that she can still say that her poetry is leading her in unpredictable directions, and to unpredictable dreams... every day.